Tales from Mu

Chapter Titles

Chapter 1.	The Ghost of A
Chapter 2.	The Sally Wattle
Chapter 3.	Blackberry picking on Mullen's Hill
Chapter 4.	The Parcel from America
Chapter 5.	Granny's Scullery
Chapter 6.	Mammy... The Arsonist
Chapter 7.	Mullen's Shop
Chapter 8.	McBennett's Shop
Chapter 9.	World War II on Mullen's Hill
Chapter 10.	McKee's Kilfie
Chapter 11.	Kate Duff – The Fish Woman
Chapter 12.	The Carberry Family of Sturgeon's Hill, Clonmore
Chapter 13.	Frank & Mary Mullen
Chapter 14.	Mammy's Little Sister – Rita Mullen Shannon
Chapter 15.	Mammy and the Two Sirs
Chapter 16.	The Perils of Serving your Time
Chapter 17.	The Stone Fire
Chapter 18.	Soda Bread making
Chapter 19.	Anne Mullen
Chapter 20.	The Ruddery Hill Pump
Chapter 21.	Miss Lizzie McNeece
Chapter 22.	George Mullen
Chapter 23.	Mullen's Hill Song
Chapter 24.	Pat Mullen & Joene
Chapter 25.	Jim Mullen
Chapter 26.	The Phone Box in Tullyroan
Chapter 27.	Lost on Mullen's Hill
Chapter 28.	The Moss's come to Mullen's Hill

*Happy reading
Barbara*

Forward

The power of storytelling, reminiscing, reflecting upon rich lives lived and vivid memories of loved ones can never be underestimated.

This book of stories is a beautiful gift of gems ....all 28, warm, tender insightful, short stories, precious recollections from a unique and much loved lady.

I first met Barbara McGahan on a Bus when we were starting out on a brave new adventure as first year pupils at St Joseph's Convent, Donaghmore... ....we have shared so many adventures ever since…a friendship spanning almost five decades.

I have very happy memories of visiting and meeting both Barbara's parents and spending time in their home. It was a privilege to know them. A home full of music and storytelling, it was always warm and welcoming. I was struck by Barbara's attention to detail and her mother's vivid stories and recollections.

This book is a tribute to her late Mother, Brigid, a true lady, a fashionista, who revelled in the company of her family, her daughter, Barbara and son, Aidan and all their family, children and grandchildren and great grandchildren… where love was palpable.

These stories provide an opportunity to embrace and celebrate these much loved memories with relish from a very special lady.

Now, just over two years after her passing, Barbara beautifully assembles this wonderful collection of "Tales from Mullen's Hill ". Embrace and enjoy this delightful experience through the eyes of a lady and a life well lived.

Huge congratulations Barbara on your beautiful and moving collection of "Tales" so charmingly brought to life from your mother's own words.

Noelle McAlinden
Creative Adviser, Artist, Curator, Educator, Arts & Human Rights Activist
& Dear Friend of many years

Tales from Mullen's Hill

Introduction

This little book is a heartfelt tribute to my late Mother, Brigid. Born in March 1924 and raised in the little enclave of Mullen's Hill, Co Armagh, right on the banks of the River Blackwater (An Abhainn Mhór - The Great River), which strides through County's Tyrone and Armagh ending up in the vast Lough Neagh – a few miles downriver. She grew up in a time of simplicity and innocence, in a rural Ireland that now lives on only in memory.

A Mullen by birth, Mammy possessed a remarkable skill for recollection. In her later years, she delighted in sharing stories from her youth, weaving tales of growing up and navigating life in the mid 1900's. Sadly, she was taken from us quite suddenly in September 2021, aged 97, a victim of the aftermath of a Covid outbreak. Had it not been for this unforeseen circumstance, she would have undoubtedly achieved the coveted milestone of "making the 100," as we often jokingly discussed with her.

In what would have been her hundredth year, I felt it fitting to gather some of her cherished recollections in this little book, creating a lasting memorial to her. My hope is that it brings joy to readers of all ages and stands as a living piece of history for her children, grandchildren, great-grandchildren, and all who turn its pages.

I dedicate this book to the Mullen family of Mullen's Hill, Co Armagh, and their many descendants. I am indebted to my Aunt, Rita Shannon of Yonkers, New York, whose equally good memory I have raided on occasion. Additionally, I fondly remember my late father, Tommy McGahan, whose gentle wit and wisdom are woven through these pages too.

Barbara Morgan

Mullen's Hill, is a tiny area which lies beside the River Blackwater at the very edge of Co Armagh and bordering on to Co Tyrone. It is recorded by this name on the Ordinance Survey Maps of 1846 where it shows a cluster of dwellings in the townland of Derrymagone, adjacent to the large country estate of the McGeough Bond Family, which was known as The Argory. The Irish word maolán refers to a bare hill and it is the same word that is used in the surname O' Maoláin - which means "decscendant of the bald or tonsured one." Mullen was a fairly common name in the area and it is imagined at one time that the area got its name from the surnames of the families who lived there who were most likely related or descendants of a large family.

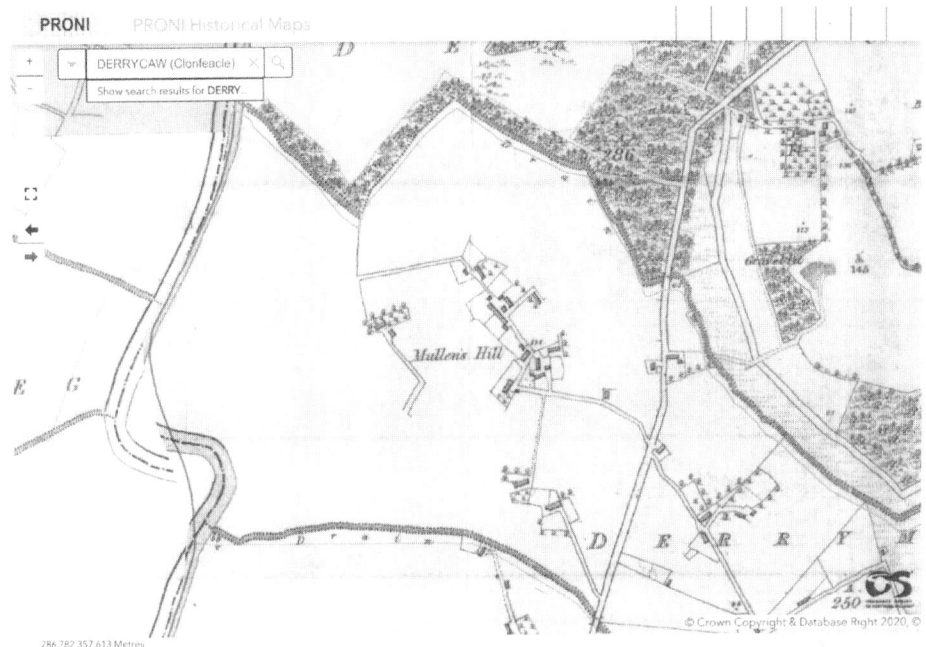

1832 - 1846 Proni Map

Thanks

My thanks go to all who have helped me with these stories. To my husband Michael and sons Ronan and Daragh, for their support, and to those further afield who have inspired and cajoled me to publish this book. For your kindness, wisdom and reassurance, I will be forever thankful. Barbara.

The Ghost of Annie Pawley

On one of my many chats with Mammy - she recalled this strange little tale which she always told us around Halloween time and as children we grew up hearing it retold every year and it always scared us - it still does!

Many moons ago, probably in the mid 1930's, when my mammy was around eight or nine years old she, along with her mother and several local women were walking back from October Devotions is St John's Chapel, Moy, late on an October evening. Mammy remembers that her own mother, Margaret Mullen, along with Rose Carberry, Lizzie McNeece and her cousins the Carberry girls, Brigid and Kathleen, were there. It would have been dark and the women were carrying battery lamps to light their way home. The girls ran on ahead probably chatting and playing and darting back to the women, when they got too far away from the safety of the lamplight. Now in the townland of Canary, which was right next door to Derrymagone, where they all were from, there lived an old lady who was well known to them, her name was Annie Pawley or Annie Polly, as we always thought she was called. She lived in a little house which had been built in a dip of land below the road on what became known locally as Polly's Hill. Annie's husband William had been a Blacksmith and there was a small forge at the side of their house. William had been a lot older when he married the young Annie Murray - he was 71 and a widower - to her 30 years. They had no children and William had died in 1920, after they had been married fifteen years. Mammy remembers Annie as a pleasant old lady - who kept herself to herself and who lived for many years on her own. It was well known to them all that Annie had died some weeks prior to that night and had lain in the little house for a few days before her body was discovered.

As the party of women and girls made their way towards Polly's Hill, Mammy and the young Carberry girls, ran on ahead and even though it would have been a dark evening, they could clearly see the figure of Annie Pawley walking down the hill towards them from her former home. Mammy said they felt no fear at all, even though they knew that she had died and been buried a few weeks earlier. The girls ran back to the women and told them that they had seen the ghost of Annie Pawley, again no fear was expressed by anyone and the women all linked arms and walked on towards Polly's Hill. Sure enough within a few strides they too could see the ghostly figure of Annie Pawley making her way towards them. Mammy said that Annie had a very calm expression and took no notice of them but walked through the group and down the hill and disappeared into the night. The women, good people that they were, surmised that she was making her way back to her former childhood home which was in Tullyroan - another neighbouring townland and that they should pray for peace for her soul, which they did, reciting prayers for Annie as they made their way home.

As children we were always scared to walk past the house on Polly's Hill and would look away from the old house every time we went by in case we would see Annie looking out!.. Of course we never did... but the story was ingrained in our memories and is a little piece of a forgotten time. I do hope that Annie and her husband William rest easy and that their souls and the souls of all the good gentle people of that time and place are all at peace.

The Sally Wattle

When we were children growing up in Derrymagone the main dispenser of discipline was always our mother. She laid down the law and gave out the punishments no matter what. I never remember my Father Tommy ever raising his hand to us - and God knows he probably could have done many times. Mammy, on the other hand was the one for that. Not that she ever smacked us - no she had a much more effective means of punishment - The Sally Wattle. We lived in fear of the swish of the Sally Wattle - the sharp sting of it on the backs of our legs, where it seemed to hurt just that little bit more. Don't get me wrong, we were not over punished or beaten to death with it - but we knew when Mammy reached for it that we were in big trouble.

The Sally Wattle was a thin sapling branch of ash, which Mammy would cut out of the local hedgerows, she would then strip off most of its leaves, - just a few at the top - kept for extra air flow and speed!!! and this was then placed at the side of the kitchen range fire - to dry out - and make it even sharper and stingier!!! One would usually last a few weeks before breaking in two from the heat of the fire. Mammy would then make a bit of a ceremony by announcing to us that she was "Away out to the hedge to cut a new Sally Wattle!". Whilst we had been delighted when the current Sally Wattle had broken..... we were always hopeful that it would not be replaced... but we were always disappointed. We would plead with Mammy to cut a big one as we knew the wider the sapling the less likely it was to sting.... sadly Mammy had an eye for selecting the thinnest most flexible sapling and thus another Sally Wattle made its home beside our fire ready to keep The McGahan children in line.

Just the thought of it waiting quietly in the corner of the kitchen was enough to keep me and my brother in check and maybe Mammy knew that all too well.

Blackberry Picking
on Mullen's Hill

While chatting with my mother one afternoon... the subject of making jam came up…... and we were remembering all the lovely jams she used to make for us, strawberry, gooseberry, raspberry, damson plum, rhubarb and ginger and her favourite, victoria plum. I remarked that the hedgerows are currently full of lovely ripening blackberries and she told me this lovely story.

At this time of the year, Mammy and her brothers and sisters would be sent out around the local hedgerows in and around Derrymagone and Mullen's Hill, Co Armagh to gather blackberries. It was not for her mother to make jam with though - they were sold to a travelling salesman who came around the country on a donkey and cart selling bits and pieces and collecting various fruit which he used to make jam. His surname was Farrell. It was essential that the Mullen children collected enough blackberries to enable their parents to buy wooden clogs for them all to wear over the winter. So they were very busy and enjoyed collecting the fruit, but it was hard work for small children. The wooden clogs were bought in Hobson's shop in the Moy and they had a laced up leather top - so only the soles were wooden. Mammy said when they were new they could be very slippery and were great for sliding about on the icy roads. Her father nailed a piece of rubber to the sole of each of the clogs to give them a better grip. The Mullen children(George, Brigid, Nan, Pat, Jim and Rita) walked three miles to school each day in Clintyclay, Clonmore and three miles home again - so hardy footwear was essential. The clogs were not very pretty but they were comfortable and were worn by many of the local children. Mammy distinctly remembers getting her first pair of leather soled shoes when she was about twelve or thirteen - that would have been around 1936. She loved them as they were tan in colour and so light and smart and she was so pleased with them - they still bring a smile to her face even all these years later and indeed she always had a liking for nice shoes... and homemade jam… something she has passed on to me too!

The parcel from America

Mammy often remembers that from time to time her mother would receive a much welcomed parcel from America. It most likely came from her Father's Uncle - James Mullen, who had emigrated to New York and by all accounts - "done quite well". He had a Grocery shop and a Bar and a large family of seven children. The parcel usually contained hand me downs from James' children, who were a little older than Mammy and her brothers and sisters. One such parcel arrived and among the various items of clothes were a gaudy pair of red, pointed toed, shoes. Unfortunately for Mammy - she had the only feet that fitted these shoes and so her mother announced that they would be a great pair of shoes for school!!!. And the very next day Mammy was sent off to school wearing the offending shoes.

Now to say she didn't like them would have been an understatement. Even in those long ago days my mother had a sense of style about her and "Yankee, red, pointy toed, shoes" certainly did not fit the bill and would not have gone down well among her schoolmates at Clintyclay Primary School. However woe betide trying to refuse to wear them and so with a heavy heart off she plodded in the accursed! shoes. However, Brigid was not to be outdone and as she walked off to school through "The Plantin" or The Argory, as it is better known now, she came up with the idea that she would simply take off the dreadful shoes - hide them behind a bush at the black gates and proceed on to school barefoot. I have asked her was that a strange thing to do -- but she assured me that it wasn't, and that many of the children would have been barefoot at school in those times. All was well until a huge downpour came on whilst she was at school. She realised that the shoes, which she had hidden, would be soaked through... which indeed they were. Mammy - like the good child she was, put on the soaking wet shoes on the way home from school and arrived at home as if nothing had happened. Her mother - my granny Margaret, was not one bit slow and probably heard the squelching from the sodden shoes - needless to say there were stern words and probably a few tears - but Mammy never had to wear the "Yankee red shoes" again.

Granny's Scullery

My Grandmother Margaret - neé Carberry - who was born on Sturgeons Hill, in Clonmore, in 1896, was a wonderful cook and a very proud housekeeper. She kept her little house on Mullen's Hill as neat as nine pence. However with six children - three boys and three girls, all growing up in their small cottage home, she found that the space was getting a little tight. She was a great planner and was always after her husband James to enlarge the house or to make improvements. James was an excellent craftsman and carpenter, who could turn his hand to almost anything, but, like the cobbler whose children didn't have shoes - he didn't spend a lot of time working on his own house. This caused quite a bit of tension in the Mullen home, as you can imagine. However, Granny, ever resourceful, decided that she would take matters into her own hands and so one day she got her three boys, who were barely into their teens - George, Jim and Pat, to knock a hole in the back of the kitchen mud wall, which would lead into the new kitchen scullery that Granny had wanted for a long time. When my Grandfather returned from work that day there was a gaping hole in the back of his house!!... it was one of the very few occasions that James Mullen was known to have sworn….. but there was no turning back and James had to take the next few days to build on the tiny scullery which was such a dream of my Grandmothers and which stood solid and well for many years and which I remember fondly from my childhood too. It was cool in summer - and in winter it was freezing!! But it was where my Grandmother baked and cooked and eventually my Mother and my Aunt Anna Mullen too. There was always a wonderful smell of something just about to be baked or just coming out of the oven and I'm sure it brought much pleasure to my Granny and the other Mullen women who made good use of it over the years. I'm also sure that the good gentle James Mullen didn't for one moment regret that he had a strong wife who could take matters into her own hands when need be.

Mammy the Arsonist

This little story only came to light several years ago when we were all sitting having dinner with my cousin Charlie Shannon, who is a Fire Fighter in the Bronx, New York. I don't know if it was us talking about his job - but Mammy suddenly stunned us all with this little memory.

Many years ago, when my mother was a teenager, she had come home from work (she was an apprentice shop assistant in Hobson's of Moy), and she decided that she would light up the hearth fire and get the dinner ready for her father and brothers and sisters returning from work later that evening. Her Mother had gone to stay with her sister Mary, for a few days - so Mammy was "in charge". She had raked up the dead ashes - as she had done many times before and went out to throw them on the dunghill, as was the custom. She went back into the house to get a pan of water to dampen them down, but something had distracted her and she forgot all about doing this all important thing. It was to have huge repercussions.

Her father James, a carpenter, was working on a roof of a house in Tullyroan, which is a nearby townland - approximately three miles away. It was a clear summer day and he noticed a plume of smoke rising in the distance. He said to the men working with him - "I think that is coming from the direction of my house" and immediately came down from the roof and made his way back home in great haste, on his bicycle. He was correct - the smoke was coming from his yard - a spark from the "dead ashes" had blown across the yard and lit one of the two large haystacks which had just been gathered in and stacked side by side in the farmyard. This was bad enough, as the hay was to feed the animals over the winter, but even worse the small farmhouse was roofed in thatch, which was highly flammable and was on the verge of catching fire too.

Mammy remembers that the neighbours came from all around - from Derrymagone, Canary, The Ruddery, and some from Tullyroan and Copney. The men formed a chain, drawing water from the well at the bottom of Mullen's Hill and passing buckets up the lane to the farm yard and back again. The local women, fearing that the house would catch alight, managed to hold a large tarpaulin over the side of the house to protect the thatch from the flames. They held this in place for four hours until the last sparks of the fire in the yard had been extinguished and the house was safe. Both stacks of hay were lost.

What a wonderful feat of resourcefulness, neighbourliness and community. How they all came together to try to save a family's home and their precious hay. There would have been no point in sending for a fire brigade, as someone would have had to go into Dungannon to arrange for it to come out.... by which time it would have been too late.

I asked Mammy what her father's reaction was to the fire. She said, he was a very gentle, kind hearted man and he said " Sure it wasn't the lassies fault... she was only trying to do her best for us all". What a lovely response from him... she has never forgot it.

I never got the chance to meet him, but just by those few words I know I would have liked him.

Mullen's Shop

Many people still remember Mullen's shop which lay at the foot of Mullen's Hill in Derrymagone, Co Armagh. It was originally run by my great grandparents, George & Eliza Mullen and was carried on after their deaths by their only daughter Annie. (Born 26 January 1896 - died 29 August 1984).

The shop and meal yard was run primarily by Eliza, who was a formidable lady with a good head for business and figures. Her husband George was an Inspector for the Ministry and took very little to do with the shop and meal business. They lived there with their five children, James, Annie, Georgie, Frank and Barney.

Eliza was from Derryhohan, in Clonmore and her maiden name was also Mullen, it is said that when a woman does not change her name upon marriage that she is granted a "cure" and Eliza was said to have the "cure" for whooping cough because of this.

My mother remembers her grandparents clearly and has told me that Granda Mullen was a gruff man, who always walked with a limp - she remembers that while he was not very tolerant of his little grandchildren, he would always have his pockets full of mint sweets, which he would scatter on the ground for them to scrabble for, maybe that was one way of keeping them busy and quiet!!

Their only Daughter, Annie, took over the running of the shop and yard when her parents died and over the years it became the hub of the small local community. Annie ruled over the shop and everyone who came into it with a rod of iron... the adage "the customer is always right" had no meaning for Annie and you ran the risk of offending her in numerous ways when calling at the shop.

In order to gain entry to the shop - which was a room in the middle of the house - you had to come into the porch and knock on the kitchen door - Annie would peep out from the diamond shaped window in the porch and depending on several things, would deem to serve you in the shop. Her number one offence was to call when the wrestling was on the television on a Saturday afternoon... you had absolutely no chance of her coming to the door and woe betides if you tried to knock and walk into the kitchen - you would be sharply told to come back later. She could be heard loudly egging on the wrestlers and counting them out... one ah... two ah... three ah!!! as they writhed in the ring.

She would also never respond to anyone knocking for the shop if she had visitors - which she did quite often. Annie was a well-read woman and loved to discuss and debate with anyone who would give her a good argument. She completed the Irish News crossword each day and posted in her results - winning too, on many occasions. One of her crossword companions was local gentleman Sir Walter McGeough Bond of The Argory - he called frequently with her and they spent hours puzzling over the crossword clues and apparently even more time arguing over who would pay for the penny stamp to post in the entry!!

The other major offence was to appear at the door inappropriately dressed. Now bear in mind that when I would have been sent down to Annie's shop - it was in the mid-sixties, and we lived in rural Ireland where the fashion stakes were not really at the cutting edge. On one occasion I was sent down to the shop for something and I was wearing my new, turquoise corduroy shorts - it was summer - I was about seven!. Annie peered around the kitchen door and asked what I was wearing.... .....I being ever the fashionista!! - said "They're Hot Pants!!" She nearly exploded and said, "Go back to your mother and ask her to dress you in more appropriate clothing for a young lady - if ye knew the meaning of those words you'd not be allowed out in those things". Suitably chastised I traipsed back home and related the offence to Mammy … she was not impressed - but I always had to be checked and dressed properly before being sent to the shop after that.

The shop in Annie's time supplied basic commodities, bread, sugar, flour, potatoes, stamps, parrafin for Tilly lamps and mantles too, boiled sweets, milk and butter (there was no refrigerator - so these were stored on the stone floor at the back of the shop) and of course the obligatory cigarettes. Annie did a great trade in these and always had a large selection of smokes - the overflow she stored in a big cupboard in the kitchen. The shop was dark with lots of little cubby holes and shelves - I loved to explore them but I always knew to keep an eye out for Annie who did not tolerate "wee childer" rummaging through her shop. The wooden counter was covered with red linoleum which was smooth and lovely to touch as it had taken on the grain of the wood over the years.

Her banking method was also unusual in that her main mode of saving money was to stash it in between the pages of "The Far East" or the "Africa" magazines which she kept on an old ships chair which sat in the kitchen. The thinking being that the "Holy" magazines would take care of the money and sure no one would steal from them.... I'm not sure that was always the case and I'm sure a few fly boys managed to slip out a few pound notes when she was not looking. When she had a surplus of money she would move to the more secure banking facility which was an old biscuit tin which she would tie up in the branches of one of the apple trees in the orchard behind the shop. This worked quite well, until on one occasion the rain got into the tin and soaked all the paper notes... Annie brought them in and laid them out to dry on the open hearth fire in the kitchen, which was always kept lit. All was going well until a neighbour called and their large dog ran into the kitchen and managed to gobble up most of the drying notes.....a costly event... which caused much dispute about who was responsible...Not sure it was ever resolved!.

The photo below is of Mullen's shop - taken around 1930. She shop was the window to the left of the front door... the sign says "Players Please".

Annie never married and lived out all of her 88 years in the shop and house she called home. She carried on with the shop right into the early 1980's and it never really closed fully until she passed away. The house is still there, now lived in by one of my cousins but I imagine that the spirit of those strong Mullen women, Eliza and Annie lives on in many of us.

McBennett's Shop

While Mullen's Hill was not quite the centre of the universe - it was quite the spot... and even though Annie Mullen's shop stocked a variety of just about everything and anything..If you could manage to gain entry!! - About half a mile up the road in the townland of Canary, there was another shopping emporium which held much fascination for us when we were children. For unlike Annie's, McBennett's shop was a bright airy place, run by Sean and Veronica McBennett, where the ever pleasant, cheerful and lovely Mrs McBennett (Veronica) would most often serve you. McBennett's had the untold luxury of rows of gorgeous mouth-watering sweets stacked in jars behind the counter. Great patience was shown to all us local children who often took a long time to choose their sweets... which were then weighed ceremoniously on a large set of white scales, with us watching to see if we could squeeze another gob stopper or brandy ball into the bag!! Very often Veronica and Sean would throw a few extra in the bag....to our utter joy.

The shop also would have had lovely cakes and buns, if my memory serves me right, also a freezer, with ice lolly's and they also served the most wonderful ice cream sliders - which still make my mouth water and which of course were a great treat for us.

Sean McBennett, Veronica's husband (born 11 April 1918 and died 10 March 2001), drove a mobile shop around the local area travelling as far away as Maghery and Stewartstown, on his rounds. For many rural, housebound women and their children, the arrival of the "shop" was a highlight of the week. They would have bought supplies for the week, fresh bread, vegetables, the weekly newspaper and maybe, if lucky, a treat or two in the form of a sticky bun or cake.

We called regularly at McBennett's - always on the outlook for Aunt Annie - who didn't look favourably on us frequenting the "opposition".

When you called to the shop you rang a bell at the door - it rang inside the McBennett's home house, which was just across the yard. Most times Mrs McBennett or Sean would come out and you could be sure that along with your purchases you would have the chance to chat over "important "local and even world-wide events. There was no sense of hurry and the conversation was as much a key part of the transaction as the purchase! Sometimes the McBennett children would come out to serve in the shop - a job we looked upon with envy. The children, John, Dolores, Patsy, Brendan and Collette were all images of their parents and had the same friendly manner. My father had a fondness for Dolores who was a very pretty young girl... he used to call her Delicious... which always made us giggle.

The other important service that the McBennett family provided was that they had, in the front hallway of their home, the only telephone in the neighbourhood for many miles. This was where you made calls to family members far away - where you conveyed or received news of deaths, of births or of marriages. This was how you checked up on people who were in hospital and how you made important appointments. It is impossible to convey to young people now - who never have their phones out of their hands - how valuable a service that was. It was not abused and every phone call was discussed and considered before "going to McBennett's'" to make the call.

Mrs McBennett passed away on 27 December 1997. McBennett's shop was in operation from 1962 until it closed on 9 March 2001 - the day before Sean passed away. Sean worked in the shop himself until a few months before his passing aged 83.

Below are some photographs of the shop and the McBennett home and a great photo of Sean behind the counter.

World War II at Mullen's Hill

I was chatting to my Aunt Rita Shannon recently and she recounted these very interesting and moving memories of the war years that she remembers from her time growing up in Mullen's Hill.

In the very early years of World War Two, there were both British and Belgian soldiers stationed at The Argory and Derrygally House, which were large country estates very near to Mullen's Hill, these estates were owned and lived in by the McGeough Bond family. American soldiers were stationed at The Argory towards the end of the war.

Rita remembers the young soldiers and in particular the battle manoeuvres and drills which they enacted in the field behind her home house and across the road in Crossey's field. She said that these took up most of the day and upwards of 40 young men would be lying on their stomachs in the field and up against the hedges, in full battle gear, in all weathers, with the Officers shouting out instructions. Rita and her family also grew used to the sight of a huge army tank parked right in front of their front door for most of the day, with a soldier sitting in the turret. Rita said it made a trip to the outside toilet an adventure - to say the least!

Her mother would be baking soda bread which she made on the griddle over the open hearth every day. One day an Officer came to the door and asked if a few of the men could have some of the home-made bread. My grandmother agreed and this became a ritual with the Officer bringing four or five of these young lads in to the kitchen at a time for tea and home-made soda bread straight off the griddle and smothered in home-made butter, which would have been churned in the house by my grandmother Margaret.

My poor grandmother could hardly keep up with their appetites and as soon as she took one bannock of soda off the griddle - it was eaten. The Officer was very polite and once one group was finished he would ask could he bring another group in. He brought different lads each time over the period of several weeks so that nearly everyone got a turn.

Although there was very little interaction between the young soldiers and the locals at that time, my Grandmother felt for these young lads and it became a ritual that when they were lying in the fields during these day long manoeuvres she would send my Aunt Rita up through the drills with a croc of hot sugared tea. The soldiers would hold out their enamel mugs - while still lying flat on the ground - and Rita would tip the croc of hot tea into the cups moving up and down the drills of men until they all had some tea. The reason Rita was sent was that she was only small - she was aged about 7 or 8 - and she could move easily through the drills without being seen by the Officers, who would not have allowed the men to have tea while on these manoeuvres.

A neighbour challenged my Grandmother about giving tea to the soldiers and she responded by saying - "I've three boys myself and I'd like to think that if they were in some foreign land, preparing to go to war, someone would show them a bit of kindness too". Doesn't that show what a kind and loving person she was - a typical Irish mother.

Rita remembers that the young soldiers would march in formation into the Moy each evening, going there via Canary and coming back via Derrygally - a route of about ten miles. Once this march was completed they had some free time and they would often make their way up to Mullen's shop where they were able to buy cigarettes and maybe sweets too. It became a bit of a social hub and they enjoyed talking with Annie Mullen who was a well-read young woman and who always kept abreast of the world news, especially relating to the war.

These young soldiers knew that they were preparing to go to the front and that their time in Derrymagone/Mullen's Hill was a bit of a rest and a holiday before they went to war. Rita remembers that the night before their unit was leaving for the front many of the young men were very distressed and some were in tears..... It must have been a frightening prospect for them and indeed some of them would never return.

Before they left they brought up boxes of tinned goods, fruit, custard, etc. which they left in a huge pile at the front of Mullen's shop, with instructions that this should be shared out among the neighbours - they particularly asked that the lady who made the lovely soda bread should get some.

The photographs below show some details of the British and Belgian Army at The Argory and a photograph of an army tank of that time.

I've also included a copy of a Ration Book which is dated 16 October 1939 and you can see clearly the various stamps for Meat, Bacon & Ham, Butter & Margarine, Cooking Fats, including Lard & Dripping and Sugar - all items which were rationed.

McKee's Kilfee

Growing up on Mullen's Hill we were blessed with lovely neighbours. Our closest neighbours were Paddy and Mary McKee who lived right next door to us. The McKee's were an old Derrymagone family and indeed they had married into the Mullen clan on more than one occasion too. Paddy was the youngest of the seven children of Patrick McKee and Elizabeth Mackle - he was born on 4 May 1910. He married Mary Mulholland of Portadown and they had four children, Joe, Eamon (RIP), Gertie and Tommy. Mammy remembers the McKee lads as being full of spirit and she recalls Eamon swimming across the Blackwater River with his little brother, Tommy, on his back. Eamon went on to join the Irish Army and sadly died a young man. He is buried in Glasnevin Cemetery, Dublin.

At the side of McKee's house was a tree covered passage which winded its way along the side of their property and around the back of our barn and acted as a sort of a short cut or thoroughfare from the back of Mullen's Hill. It shortened the route for those walking up or down the hill. It was always known locally as "McKee's Kilfee". It may be from an Irish word "cúlbhealach" meaning backway or by-way. I don't know where the name "Killfee" comes from or how it should be spelt. The "Kilfee" is still there, although a little overgrown and not used much nowadays..... Maybe it would be a good idea to begin using it again.

The recent photographs are of the "Kilfee" and also of the old McKee house which is now empty, but still a very beautiful spot... all I could hear were the birds singing in the trees.

Kate Duff - the Fish Woman

Mammy often remembered an old woman named Kate Duff, who walked around the area selling fresh fish. Kate was from Maghery, Co Armagh, which is about ten miles from Mullen's Hill, and she walked from there round the country roads with the fish in a wooden riddle, which she carried on her head. She had her customers in each area and did a good trade in selling fresh fish. They were mostly Pullen or Mackerel. Mammy said that, as children, her brothers and sisters were always fascinated at how she managed to balance the fish container on her head.

The photograph below shows Kate at the back door of The Argory, where she also sold her fish. The man is Secondo Banducci, an Italian man who was Valet to Sir Walter McGeough Bond. The photograph was taken in 1934.

I was contacted recently by a great grandson of Kate Duff's. He was able to tell me a little bit more about Kate. She was born just outside Stewartstown in around 1860 and came from a poor family. She found work in Maghery selling fresh fish and would have walked as far as Dungannon town with her fish. It is known that she would stop at the Fish Ponds, near Tamnamore, in order to refresh her fish in the

clear running waters of the Fish Ponds, before going on to Dungannon for the Market Day. She died in 1944, aged around 84 and is buried in Maghery Graveyard.

It is wonderful to think of the many miles she must have walked and the homes she visited over the years as she made her way selling her fresh fish between Maghery and Dungannon.

The Carberry's of Sturgeons Hill, Clonmore

A few people have contacted me regarding the Carberry's who were my Grandmother Margaret's family. They lived in a small farm at the top of Sturgeon's Hill in Clonmore. Apparently it got its name as the home of one of the Land Stewards for the nearby Verner Estate was called Mr Sturgeon and he lived in a large house on the hill, which then took on his surname. The house, I believe, was called Clintyclay House.

The Carberry family consisted of Mammy's grandfather, James, his wife Brigid - who was formerly Loughran of Galbally and their children, Mary, Patrick, Johnny, James, Annie, Sarah and Margaret- who was my grandmother.

The eldest girl Mary married Hugh Donaghy of Derrytresk on Valentine's Day 1901 and despite the romantic day went on to have a sad life. Her husband injured his foot on a spade while cutting turf - this then turned septic and he died in January 1902. Mary gave birth to their first child in April 1902 a little girl also called Mary. Sadly the baby died in February 1903 aged 10 months from Measles and Pneumonia. So within the space of just over a year Mary had been married, widowed, given birth and lost her only child - she was only 23. Mary never married again and lived for a while in Ravensdale, Co Louth before coming back to Dungannon and setting up a Confectioner and Newsagent shop in Scotch Street, Dungannon. Mammy remembers Mary as being a cross, sharp lady - but given her life, maybe that's explainable.

The boys Patrick and Johnny never married and lived all their days in Clonmore carrying out an egg collection and delivery business. Mammy remembers helping out as a child by washing the eggs before they could be taken on to market. She said they had a beautiful horse which drew the cart carrying the eggs and other farm produce which they sold. In her words "that horse was treated better than any Christian", by which she means that they treated the horse with great kindness and he was much loved. Their brother James married Rose Campbell of Collegeland and had four children, twins - Catherine Winifred and James Joseph, (he died aged 8 months), Brigid and James Felix. Their sister Annie lived with her parents and the other sister Sarah died aged 12. Mammy's mother Margaret was the youngest and she of course married James Mullen of Mullen's Hill.

As a young child Mammy was sent down to help at her grandmothers and lived there on and off for several years, as was the custom at that time. She had to work very hard for her Aunt Annie who kept the house and farm yard spick and span. She loved her uncles Paddy and Johnny and said they were great craic. Mammy often remembered all the beautiful china and glass which her grandmother had in the "breakfast room". One particular memory which still stays with her is of her Aunt Annie, clearing out some of the delph and china which was deemed "no longer fashionable". She would bundle the items into a bag and send Mammy along the lane which led down to the River Blackwater with the instructions to pitch the whole lot into the river!!. Mammy remembers all the beautiful stuff which was thrown away and often says that they must be somewhere at the bottom of the river even yet......

To the left is a photograph of Sturgeon's Hill, showing Clintyclay House in the foreground with Carberry's farm and house to the left behind it.

The Carberry Jug??

A few weeks after writing this story a local lady contacted me and over the last number of days she has kindly given me a little jug which she found on the banks of the River Blackwater, in Clonmore, after it was dredged some years ago. Miraculously the little jug is entirely intact.....could it be part of the treasure trove of delph and china that my mother "pitched" into the river all those years ago (nearly 90 now) ? Who knows..... But what a lovely thought

Frank & Mary Mullen

The wedding photograph below, of a very handsome couple, is my great uncle, Frank Mullen and his wife, Mary, neé Fay. Mary was from a townland called Derrydamph in Co Cavan and Frank, of course, was born and reared in Mullen's Hill, Co Armagh. I don't know what sent the two of them across the sea to New York - Mary possibly went to an older sister who was already there and Frank possibly travelled with his brother Barney who also lived there.

Mary and Frank married in New York in 1940. Frank always said they courted for twelve years before they could afford to get married. Life was tough in New York in the 1930's during the Great Depression and Frank often told how he and his brother Barney had to queue at soup kitchens just to get some food to eat.

They did eventually have a very happy and comfortable life in the Bronx - however it was always Frank's dream to return home to Mullen's Hill and build a retirement home for them both. I don't think Mary was as keen on the move, but back they came in 1964 and built a very tidy bungalow at the bottom of Mullen's Hill. Sadly Frank only got to enjoy his retirement for a few years as he passed away suddenly in 1967. Mary lived on for another 36 years in their little home. She travelled back and forward to New York many times - always "threatening" to retire back there - but that never did happen. Instead she lived out her life in the middle of the Mullen family who cared for her with great fondness and were always in awe of her "American Ways", not to mention her legendary appetite!!

Mary died peacefully aged 93 in 2003.

I often look at their beautiful wedding photograph, where they stand full of love and hope for their future and I like to think that they are once again happily together and that they would be quietly delighted that they are still remembered with great fondness here on Mullen's Hill.

Mammy's Little Sister – Rita Mullen Shannon

My aunt Rita Shannon (Margaret Mary Mullen) celebrates her birthday on -1 April. She and Mammy were such special sisters and remained close even though they lived in different parts of the world for over sixty years.
With seven years between them it would seem that Mammy was always her champion - well nearly always.

Mammy recalls that when Rita was a baby she was put in charge of minding her for an afternoon - God knows, probably to give my grandmother Margaret a wee bit of a break as Rita was the youngest of six. Mammy duly took Rita out in her pram - she was a few months old and Mammy would have been about seven. Anyway, for some strange reason Mammy pushed the pram with Rita tucked up on board, up to the top of Mullen's Hill and........... let it go!!!

The pram whizzed down the very steep hill, past the Mullen home and ended up embedded in the hedge at the corner, just before the main road. Thankfully baby Rita was still intact and still inside the pram although it ended up on its side. Of course there was a hullaballoo and when questioned as to why she let the pram hurtle down the hill, Mammy replied "I wanted to see how far she could go!" No doubt there was a warm backside that evening.

Still, it didn't put Mammy off and she redeemed herself several years later when Rita began school in Clintyclay PS. The teacher of the Infant class was a very cross lady called Miss Igoe and she was well known for the severity of her slaps. Rita had fallen foul of her one day and received some of the stinging slaps on her hand... Mammy charged in from the "senior" room and told Miss Igoe, in no uncertain terms, never to slap her sister again... and I don't think she ever did! Good for you Brigid.

The pair of them remained close all their lives - even when Rita went to live in New York long years ago. Many a photo has been exchanged and telephone calls and visits made over the years and thankfully we are very close with our Shannon cousins too. Mammy enjoyed hearing news about Rita and her family and loved to remark on how well her little sister looks. The two of them are like peas in a pod - even more so as the years have passed.
"Sisters sprout from the same garden... but blossom and grow in their own way."

Brigid, Nan, Rita, Jim, Pat & George Mullen and Rover the dog
- taken in front of Mullen's shop in approx. 1934.

Rita & Brigid - taken in 2014.

Mammy and the two "Sirs"!!

When my mother was a young child she walked the three miles to the local school, Clintyclay Primary School, in Clonmore, along with her brothers and sisters and the other local children. It is a pleasant walk which takes you through the beautiful Argory Estate; indeed many times I walked to school myself along the same roads. Mammy often recalled that as they walked their weary way home from school they would be met along the road by the "Two Sirs" as she called them. These gentlemen were the local Landowner, Sir Walter McGeough Bond and his Valet, who was an Italian man by the name of Secondo Banducci. Mammy and the other children thought that Secondo was actually "Sir Condo" and they referred to them as Sir Walter and Sir Condo! The two Sirs!.

Sir Walter was a much travelled man - he had been a High Court Judge in the Court of Appeal in Cairo, Egypt, for many years and he had a great ear for languages. It is said that he was fluent in fourteen languages -including Arabic and Irish! Apparently he had travelled to the Aran Islands and stayed there for several months to perfect his Irish language skills. However to Mammy and the other children he was the much feared and very stern local "Man from the Big House".

Sir Walter would call the children over to him and get them to sit down on one of the many grassy banks along the roadside - he would sit with them too, as would Secondo. Then to their horror... he would ask to see their copy books and he would go over with them whatever they had been taught in school that day. He would also insist that they recite their prayers in English, in Latin and in Irish... and he would correct them quite severely if they made any mistakes. Needless to say they were in awe of him as little children like them did not engage with the likes of Sir Walter... or "Sir Condo". He would also ask them to learn poems and passages from the Bible, which they were expected to be able to recite to him in the following days.

Even in her late 90's Mammy could still recite the passage which she says she learned from Sir Walter - it begins:
"The Cares of Royalty
How many thousand of my poorest subjects
Are at this hour asleep! O sleep, O gentle sleep,
Nature's soft nurse, how have I frighted thee,
That thou no more wilt weigh my eyelids down

And steep my senses in forgetfulness?...."
And it continues for some twenty lines. It is a passage from Henry IV - Part II by William Shakespeare and she knew it word for word... some ninety years later. I don't know if that is due to Sir Walter's teaching or Mammy' good recall but either way it's impressive.

The photograph below is of a portrait of Sir Walter McGeough Bond of The Argory.

The Perils of Serving your Time!!

For three years, from the age of 15, my Mother "Served her Time" as a trainee shop assistant in Messrs W F Hobson, Draper and House Furnisher, Killyman Street, Moy. – Approx. 1939 to 1941.

She received no wages during this time, but at the end of the three years she was given a Post Office Savings Book with 10 shillings in it. She said that "Old Mr Hobson", as he was referred to, was very strict but fair and she enjoyed working for the Hobson family. They were Quakers and lived out the Dungannon Road, near The Grange.

I asked Mammy how she came to work there and she remembered that her Mother had asked Mr Hobson for the apprenticeship as she felt it was a good clean job, which, after the time had been served, would lead to more opportunity and better wages. Her Mother always dealt in Hobson's, as it was the main shop in The Moy for clothes and household goods.

Mammy remembers that they were always addressed very formally – Miss Mullen, Mr Kenneth etc. She remembers Fanny and Lily Gilmour and Noel Farmer and Brigid Carberry (her cousin) who worked along with her there. The ladies wore uniforms of dark green dresses with white lace collars and cuffs. These were made to measure by a woman named Mrs Brannigan in Blackwatertown.

One of Mammy's duties as the shop junior was to wash the shop windows every day – a job she didn't like, especially in the colder months. One morning, as she was washing away and whistling to herself, Old Mr Hobson called her into this office and said "A Whistling maid and a crowing hen bring bad luck all day – so please stop your whistling this minute!!" It was one telling off that Mammy never forgot, and she often referred to it. Strangely, I never knew her to whistle again.
The shop staff ate their lunch in Hetty Robinson house, which is where Dr Hobson used to live at the corner of the Square.

Mammy remembers that one of their most glamorous customers was Dr F C Wright's daughter –gorgeous hats were ordered in especially for this young lady, whom Mammy said was very beautiful. Another customer that she remembered fondly was an elderly local man who always did the clothes shopping for his wife – who never came into the shop herself. The staff had much difficulty in selecting the correct size and shape of garments from the strange descriptions and measurements – mostly hand signals!! given by this old fellow – Mammy often laughed about this. The run up to Christmas was a very busy time and they would have been very hectic up to the very last minute. The shop closed at 8.00pm on Christmas Eve and then the staff had to dress the shop windows before they were allowed to go home - so that they would be ready for the Sale, which began on Boxing Day – Mammy often remembers walking home to Mullen's Hill just before midnight on Christmas Eve.

Dressing the windows was one of the parts of the job that Mammy loved and she won a prize for dressing the windows with "K shoes". She brought in a bale of hay from home and gathered leaves and branches from the fallen trees in The Argory and dressed the autumn window with a selection of "K" shoes. One of the Reps for the company happened to see the window and put it forward for a prize – which she won – getting two new pairs of "K" shoes as her prize.

Mammy remembered that every article in the shop was marked with a "secret" code that only the employees knew. This code gave them the actual price of the item, but would have been indecipherable to those buying the goods – I suppose it gave them some bargaining room. The code word that they used in Hobson's was "MACKINTOSH" which had ten letters – each one referring to the numbers 1 – 10. So something at £1, 5 shillings and 6 pence would be marked "MIN". Wasn't that clever?

Another very eventful meeting took place while Mammy worked in Hobson's. Mammy remembers a lady and her little girl coming into the shop. She said the little girl was so pretty and good and Mammy was very taken with her. She couldn't remember their surname but the little girl was called Barbara Ann and Mammy decided there and then that if she ever had a daughter that would be just the name for her –so now you know – that's how I was named.

One dark winter evening when Mammy and her cousin Brigid Carberry were walking home from their work in Hobson's, as they came along the Canary Road which crosses the River Callan, a long lonely stretch of road, they met a young Soldier, who was sadly the worse for wear. As they approached him, he rushed towards them and pulled out a knife, which he plunged into Mammy's coat. Thankfully it was winter and she had a heavy tweed coat on with several layers underneath – so the knife did no damage. The two girls were terrified and managed to run away from the soldier, who was in no fit state to run after them. They made it to the house of an old man named Quinn who lived along that road, and he saw them safely home. For the rest of their time working in the Moy, my grandfather accompanied the two girls to and from work – him on his bicycle and them walking. I asked Mammy did they not report the soldier – and she said no – her father said that he was only a young lad, most likely scared out of his wits, and who had taken too much drink and didn't know what he was doing, and thankfully no harm was done... but it is one of the Tales that she never forgot.

This is believed to be William James Hobson "Old Mr Hobson" in Mammys day working there.

The Stone Fire

My Mother often related this strange spooky little tale, particularly around Halloween which always made us a little frightened.

Many years ago in the townland of Derrymagone, a Tinker family had come to reside in one of the small local cottages, which they rented from the owners. Apparently, they were pleasant enough folk who kept to themselves and lived quietly in the midst of all the folk on Mullen's Hill for several months. They worked on the local farms and they were also dab hands at mending farm implements, spades, buckets and other metal items - I think that is where the name "Tinker" comes from.

After a number of months they made it known that they were moving on to another area, which is what they did, moving around the country, working on the land and mending farm utensils.

One morning they had just upped and left and little or no trace of them was to be found. However when the owner of the cottage went in to check it out, he was shocked to find that they had left a "Stone Fire" in the grate of the fireplace. This was a pile of dry stones which are built up inside the fireplace. It is a very old Irish curse and was used mainly around the time of the Irish Famine, when many families were cruelly evicted from their homes. It was said to bring bad luck to the dwelling and to anyone who came to live in the house. The saying goes "Not until these fires burn shall the newcomers have any good luck!"

Mammy remembers that everyone was so shocked at this, as they had been more than hospitable to the Tinker family. It was the talk of the country for many weeks and no one could understand why it had been done. There was a lot of thought put into how the curse could be reversed. Prayers were said and candles lit, however no one was ever comfortable about living in the house again and it never was used as a dwelling house after that.

It still stands, quietly alone, perhaps holding on to the curse of the Fire of Stones even yet.

Soda Bread making on Mullen's Hill

Mammy very often recalled this little episode in her childhood which gave us all a laugh.

Mammy was well used to seeing her mother Maggie turn out creamy loaf after loaf of beautiful soda bread. Made in the iron oven (a large lidded pot) which hung over the open hearth in the kitchen of their home on Mullen's Hill and eaten with home-made butter and blackberry jam. One fine day, when Mammy was about 11 years old and when her mother had gone to town, Mammy decided she would try her hand at this baking lark- which looked so easy when her mother was doing it. However no matter what way Mammy tried to produce the lovely soft creamy soda bread that had been created with such ease by her mother- hers turned out to be lumpen messes of flour and buttermilk. Knowing that her mother would not be impressed with her efforts and also the waste of precious flour and buttermilk - Mammy came up with the wonderful solution that she would go down into the field in front of their house - dig a hole and bury all of the offending attempts that she had made at baking soda bread.

This she did, and for the moment all was well.

A few days later the local Parish Priest Father Tom Soraghan called to the house, as he often did on his rounds of the parish. My Grandmother, Maggie, sat him down at the window in the kitchen and made him tea and of course a slice of her fresh soda bread. As he sat there glancing down over the fields - he became interested in the antics of the family's Sheepdog, Rover, who seemed to be burrowing and digging in the corner of the field. He mentioned this to Maggie and together they went down to see what the daft dog was doing.... only to find that Rover had found Mammy's stash of failed baking and was having a great time digging it out from the hiding place that Mammy had made for it. Mammy was summoned and a confession obtained and while her mother was a little put out, Fatherr Soraghan laughed heartily at the whole episode, which he said was made all the more comical because even Rover the dog wouldn't eat the stuff!!

Poor Mammy, she redeemed herself many times over as she became a great baker and a fine cook - her speciality..... Soda bread.

Anne Elizabeth Mullen (Nan)

Just remembering my wonderful Aunt Nan, my mother's middle sister, was born on 3 March 1926.

She was a wonderful character - full of wit and devilment. A career Nurse who worked in Harrogate, Yorkshire, Carshalton, London and then in Canada, in a spot called Red Lake, in Ontario, which was then a remote part of the world - she often referred to it as "the end of the road", because beyond that was only vast wilderness. She shared a lot of her nursing adventures with her lifelong friend Flo Frazer Houston, who also became a dear friend of the family. Nan often talked about "Red Lake" and of how she would have to fly out in a little light plane with just a pilot and a Doctor, to help deliver the native Cree and Ojibway Indian babies, whose families lived too far away to travel to the hospital……I do believe she remembered each and every one of those little ones and her time there with great fondness.

As children, we, her nieces and nephews remember her as a daredevil - always egging us on to some sort of rascality and delighting when we accomplished it!

When she lived on Mullen's Hill at the beginning of her Nursing Career, she learned to drive a nifty Lambretta Scooter and used it to go to and from her work in St Luke's Hospital in Armagh.

Much later in her life she decided to learn to drive (along with my mother!!) and the pair of them practising on the roads around Mullen's Hill were best avoided! Still, she passed her test and continued to whizz around Belfast, where she had returned to live and work as a Matron in Lady Dixon Park, Nursing Home. We all remember the hair-raising, high speed journeys on the highways and byways of most of Ireland with her, with scant regard for road signs, directions or indeed other motorists...!!

Nan had a legendary appetite - seems to be a thing in the Mullen women!! - And you were always sure of a gigantic meal and great hospitality whenever Nan was the host.

While she had an exciting career and was well travelled she returned to live near her childhood home in her later years and passed away in the midst of her family aged 77.

When I remember her I think of the laughter and the smiles and the sense of fun she had for life and for her family.

The Ruddery Hill Pump

Part of our childhood wanderings took us all over the townland of Derrymagone and very often, after a long day adventuring….when we were tired and thirsty, we would make our way to the pump at the top of The Ruddery Hill, in the townland of Derryruddery. There we could wind the large iron wheel and pump up from the dark depths of the earth, lovely cool fresh clear water. Nothing tasted better and it was something of a novelty for us to be able to quench our thirst in this way – we also would have tried to wash the most of the dirt from our hands and faces too before we came home!!... And I can still remember the sting of the cold water on my hands and face! I asked Mammy about the pump and surprisingly she remembered it actually being installed. She thinks it was in around 1930, when she was around 5 years old and I have found two newspaper articles (see photo below) which would agree with this. I asked her why the pump was put in – firstly - in such a remote rural place and secondly – why it was put at the top of quite a steep hill. Her answer explained a lot - she said the pump was a Godsend to the local womenfolk and she especially mentioned her mother Margaret being so thankful for it. I was curious why… She went on to explain that the womenfolk had the job of looking after the livestock - mostly cattle or pigs - as the men were all away working and this was seen as women's work. Of course, this was in the days before there was running water or taps in any of their homes. The women would also have tended to any crops which were planted either for harvesting as food or as feed for the animals. This meant that they would have had to draw up large buckets of water from the wells at their own homes and then carry them up the hill and down into the meadows to supply the animals and to water the crops – can you imagine how many times they would have had to go backwards and forwards doing that! The pump meant that they could easily draw the water up and they were much nearer to the fields where the water needed to be dispersed. So despite me thinking it was a curious place for a water pump – it seems that it was a much used and welcome facility and a meeting place for the local women who came to draw the fresh water.

The pump at The Ruddery Hill – or in the townland of Derryruddery – is one of at least three in the area. There is also one in Clonmore –and one in Derrymagone – which is just a little further along the same road and possibly one in Canary too. They are Artesian Well Pumps and have been sunk down to an Aquifer. An Aquifer is an underground layer of water-bearing permeable rock, rock fractures or unconsolidated materials (gravel, sand, or silt). The Ruddery Pump is quite a deep one – it is noted that it was sunk to a depth of 63 feet in one of the newspaper reports attached. I have photographs of the pump at The Ruddery and the one further along the Derrymagone Road – see below. They are no longer working but I do think it would take very little effort and a bit of time to get them back to working order. I have spoken to a man who opened up the Ruddery Pump a few years back and drew up some water, which he said was crystal clear and perfectly drinkable. Maybe a project for a local history group or indeed for Armagh City Banbridge & Craigavon Borough Council – how great would it be to see a little bit of our rural history restored and working again?

Lizzie McNeece

When we were children growing up on Mullen's Hill, one of our favourite neighbours was Lizzie McNeece. She was a lovely, cheerful, jolly wee woman with a burbling laugh and a quick wit. She was very dear to my Mother and to us children too.

Lizzie was a great cook and baker and was always introducing my Mother to new recipes. I still have her handwritten recipe for Boiled Cake (see photograph below) and I also remember one for Banana Bread - a thing unheard of in Derrymagone of the 1960's!

When we were unwell, Mammy often sent for Lizzie, who, although she had no children of her own, was a mine of useful remedies and cures and inevitably, on our recovery, was delighted to have been instrumental in the diagnosis and of course our resurrection and return to good health.

Lizzie was born on 23 December 1900 to parents, John McNeece and Mary Jane O'Brien. She had three older brothers, James, a very religious man who at one time considered becoming a Priest and who died peacefully at home in his chair, aged 71 - he was found by the Bread Man, who called to deliver the weekly bread.

Her second brother Charles died aged 22, in 1918, from the Spanish Flu.
Her third brother, James was killed in an accident at Cowdy's Bleach Mills, at Greenhall, Loughgall, in September 1930, after he fell into a vat of boiling dip. He was the factory night foreman at Cowdy's. He was aged 32.

Lizzie began to work as a scullery maid at The Argory, the nearby home of the McGeough Bond Family, when she was just fifteen years old. Her mother was not keen on her working there - but her father had just died in 1914 and the income was needed. Lizzie's mother laid down a strict rule for her daughter and it was that she could work at The Argory, but she must never spend a night there. Lizzie adhered to that rule all her life and always came home to her little house on Mullen's Hill after a long day's work at "The Big House".

Lizzie spent all her working life with the McGeough Bond family - ending up as the Housekeeper and last remaining "servant" to the family. She was very fond of the last owner of the property whom she referred to as "Mr Bond" and she worked for the family until she asked if she could retire when she was 79 years old - a career that lasted 64 years.

The family were very kind to her - Lady McGeough Bond took a great liking to Lizzie and wanted to train her up as a Lady's Maid - but Lizzie's mother would not hear of it because she knew that Lady Bond liked to travel and that Lizzie would have to go abroad with her and her mother did not want Lizzie to be too far away from home.

Mr Bond (Walter Albert Neville McGeough Bond) the last owner of the estate was also very fond of Lizzie and his response to her when she asked if she could retire was, "But Elizabeth, this is your home!" They eventually came to an arrangement and Lizzie did retire to her little home and got to enjoy her baking and her gardening.

If ever a lady had green fingers it was Lizzie and many an hour was spent with my mother discussing the merits or ailments of a particular plant. I well remember her garden, which was not big but would have done any mansion proud. Mr Bond would come every so often for afternoon tea with Lizzie and she would make sure that everything was just so for these visits which she looked forward to very much, as did he, I believe. He gave her many little gifts from his travels abroad and one which I have - it was given to Mammy after Lizzie died - is a beautiful Italian leather purse/wallet with her name embossed on the inside - see photograph below.

Although Lizzie never had any children of her own, there are many children from Mullen's Hill who remember her with great affection. She died aged 88 in her own home on Mullen's Hill and is buried with her parents and three brothers in the Moy graveyard. I often stop at her grave and remember her and the happy times we all had in the little world that we all knew as Mullen's Hill.

Boiled Cake

1 Cup Sugar
2 " Fruit
1 " Water
2 " Flour
¼ " Margarine
1 egg
1 teaspoon Baking Soda
Pinch Salt

Put Sugar + Fruit Water + Marg
into saucepan and Boil for
at least 10 minutes. then turn
out into Bowl. and let it co[illegible]
for a [illegible] minutes then add
F[illegible] egg soda + Salt + spi[illegible]
Mix [illegible] line into bakin[illegible]
tin. Bake for 1½ hrs + 2 h[illegible]

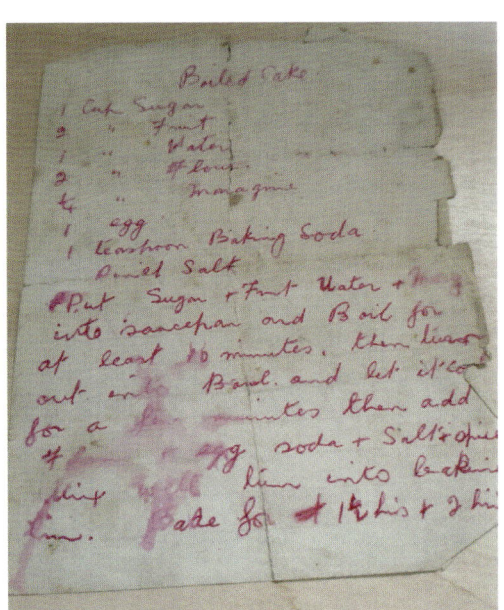

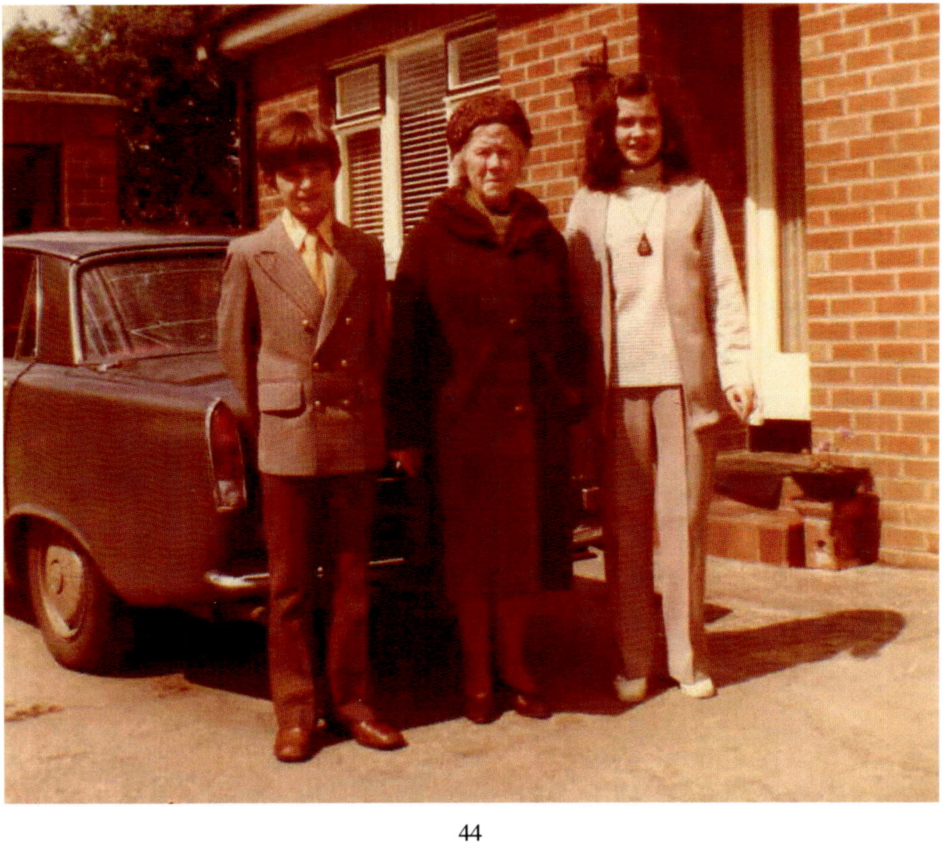

George Mullen

My Uncle George was the quiet stalwart of the family. He was Mammy's older brother, only just less than a year older than her, born 28 March 1923 and died 19 June 1997, aged 74. There was less than a year between him and Mammy – they were "Irish Twins!" and he called her by the childish name of "Bishabo".

George was a quiet unassuming person - we his family knew him as a man of little words but a very hard worker, a man whom you could call upon if you ever needed him, a man who loved watching football and who enjoyed being in company, but always on the quiet side..

One day, while out working in the fields near Mullen's Hill, he went suddenly completely blind – he was a young strapping lad of 21. Good neighbours, the Crossey's, had to walk him home as he couldn't see anything. It was a terrible blow to the family as he was a fit young man and had shown no signs of any kind of illness prior to this. He had been preparing to emigrate to the USA and plans had been set afoot for him to travel to his Uncle Frank Mullen in New York – but this blow put an end to his dreams of travelling.

His younger brother Jim Mullen became his constant companion and support at this time and it was Jim who took him to football matches and also to Mass each

Sunday in an unusual fashion. Uncle George would sit on his bicycle and rest his hand on Jim's shoulder – Jim would then pedal his own bicycle alongside George and in this way the two of them made their way around.

My aunt Rita, Uncle George's youngest sister remembers that everyone was very concerned about George and about how he must feel about the trauma of losing his sight at such a young age. The family doctor, Dr Wright of Moy, insisted that George should be included in everything as far as possible – and Jim and the rest of the family and his friends and neighbours made sure that he was never left out of anything. George and Jim remained devoted brothers all their lives.

After many tests it was determined that George had developed Eales disease. This is a disease of the eyes which affects young males in their twenties – strangely it is most prevalent in Middle Eastern countries and not rural Ireland! At that time there was no known cure for Eales disease and my Grandparents took Uncle George to see firstly the local Doctors and also to more specialised Doctors in Belfast. They also brought him to see several people who had "cures" for blindness. All was to no avail. The Doctors agreed to operate on one of his eyes in the hope of restoring some vision to it. Sadly this wasn't to be and strangely, over the next few years his sight returned to the other eye, but never to the one which was operated on.

As children we were always told that Uncle George had only one eye – but to us, despite scrutinising both his eyes whenever we got the chance – we could see no difference – both looked quite similar. George never let his partial sight impede him in any way and he was able to work and drive and he motored about the country far and wide. He worked for the local Ministry of Environment for a time and tended his small farm and his cattle and of course his moss where he cut turf for the winter months. He loved to watch football and was a great supporter of the local teams, Collegeland O'Rahilly's and Clonmore Robert Emmett's.

He was a quiet man, who didn't say much, but who took in everything. He was comfortable with his own company and that of his always present dogs, Sparky and Pip. Although George never married, he was always at all of our family events, weddings, baptisms, birthdays etc., My young cousin Patricia Shannon took a great shine to him on one of their visits to Mullen's Hill from their home in The Bronx, New York. She would plod along after George as he went about his daily farming jobs. George took little or no notice of her – but undeterred, off Patricia would go after him, walking a couple of steps behind him, like a little shadow. Many years later, in 1990, when Patricia was getting married, George surprised us all by saying he would like to go to her wedding in New York. And he did! Perhaps fulfilling that dream he had as a young man to see other places and people. He enjoyed seeing New York City and experiencing another culture and he also visited Washington where he was able to go to see Arlington Cemetery and the White House.

He would call in unannounced to many of his nieces and nephews when we grew up and married – sometimes staying just a few minutes, and sometimes taking tea and staying a while. Always willing to help or lend a hand if it was needed. It was his own gentle way of keeping in touch.

He left us quietly, aged 74. He was cared for so beautifully by his sister in law Anna Mullen and his brother Pat and he was able to spend his last few weeks in the home in which he was born on Mullen's Hill.

A day or so before he died, he made his way to the front door and stood, much as he is standing in the photograph below. He took a long look down over the fields from Mullen's Hill, down to "The Plantin", up over The Ruddery Hill and away up to Canary, and beyond into Tullyroan, perhaps remembering his childhood days growing up and the hardships he had faced…. Saying his own quiet goodbye to all that he knew and held dear on Mullen's Hill.

He is remembered for the good gentle man that he was by all of his nieces and nephews and the many neighbours and friends he had on Mullen's Hill.

Mullen's Hill Song

I was delighted to come across this beautiful song, which was composed and sung by one of our Mullen's Hill neighbours, Damien Molloy. Damien was one of the nine children of Arthur Molloy and Nan Daly, who lived across the lane from us on Mullen's Hill. Many's the time I spent in their house, with their lovely mother Nan - a joyous woman, with a twinkle in her eye and a cheerful welcome for all visitors. Her husband Arthur, who I remember chiefly for wearing his cap back to front - with the peak pointing down his back, was a quiet hard working man. Their home, although humble, was always a hive of activity with Mrs Molloy delighting in all the comings and goings... I never knew her to utter a cross word.

This lovely song reflects the beautiful childhood which we all enjoyed on Mullen's Hill.

"As I look down o'er the valley with the grass so lush and green
The Sperrin mountains in my view sure it is a lovely scene
Slieve Gullion in the distance lies and there I plainly see
Armagh's twin spires reach heaven ward in all their majesty.

That river where I offtimes fished meanders on her way
By the meadows and the woodland for to join with sweet Lough Neagh
Roxborough tower reminds me of a near forgotten day
While the fortress of Lord Charlemont slowly crumbles with decay.
As I sit here on this tranquil spot my mind is filled with ease
Looking down along the hedgerows that roll gently in the breeze
My mind begins to wander back through not so distant years
As my thoughts turn to my childhood sure my eyes they fill with tears.
For often I did roam these fields for to seek the wild birds nest
The lark the snipe and curlew they knew how to hide them best
The robin and the jenny wren to find them I knew how
And the lovely yellow hammer I so seldom see one now
I think of that once happy home I will see it never more
With its crooked walls and windows and the red tiles on the floor
Where around the turf fire on the hearth our childish games we'd play
And my mother taught me how to sing in the simple Irish way.
Now it's time that I was moving on for I'm sure that you'll agree
Life's now full of tasks and trials and responsibilities
I've enjoyed this reminiscence as my thoughts with you I've shared
I love you still that's Mullen's Hill the place where I was reared."

Many thanks to Damian Molloy for the words of this lovely song.

Uncle Pat Mullen

My Uncle Pat was the middle brother in Mammy's family. He had the quiet manner of many of the Mullen men, but was an excellent Carpenter and tradesman, like his father James, and he was a witty and pleasant man. He enjoyed Gaelic football and played for a time with Clonmore Robert Emmett's, a lifelong connection which he continued by serving for many years on the committee. He married Anna Cunningham from Lislasley, Collegelands, on 25 August 1959 and they went on to have three children, Mel, Joene and Kieran. They lived for a time in Lislasley, but after the tragic death of their little girl Joene, they moved into the Mullen family home on Mullen's Hill. We always loved going down to their home, where Anna, who was a wonderful cook and baker, always had something tasty in the oven and where everyone was always made so welcome.

They say that tragedy and sadness visits every family at some time, and it was indeed a heart breaking day when it was our turn.

Joene Mullen

On the last day of the year, as well as remembering all that has passed by in the year that has just gone, we always remember the sudden and tragic death of my little cousin, Joene Mullen. She was the middle child and only daughter of my Uncle Pat Mullen and his wife Anna and was a darling little thing, with an older brother Mel and a younger brother Kieran. I have clear memories of her playing with us all in our garden on Mullen's Hill. Her full name was Josephine Patricia Mary Mullen - which she loved to remind everyone - but she was always known as Joene. On New Year's Eve over 54 years ago the family had travelled to The Moy to do some shopping - I believe in Patterson's Shop on the Moy Hill. When they came out - Mel and Joene asked if they could run along the pavement to look into the window of McMullen's toy shop, which was a few yards along. This they did - it was a common thing for children at that time to gaze longingly at the toys in the shop window - however for some reason - Joene darted across the road - perhaps realising that her father was parked just across from the shop - on the other side of the road. Sadly an oncoming vehicle struck her a glancing blow to the side of her head. For the Mullen family, life was changed in that moment and so began a very sad and devastating time for them. Uncle Pat, who had witnessed the accident, ran from the car and picked her up -bringing her into Hobson's Chemists, which was a few doors along - but he said afterwards that he knew there was nothing which could be done. Joene died on the last day of the year in 1969 - she was just four years old. Her Father and Mother were bereft and indeed the whole family were reeling with shock.

Her brothers and all of her cousins speak about her often and remember her so fondly and although the memory is very much tinged with loss and sadness - she has been a little talisman and saintly presence in the family ever since then.

Uncle Pat and Anne have now gone to join their little daughter in Heaven, where I'm sure she was waiting for them and welcoming them with open and loving arms. As the old year ends and we all look forward to the New Year with hope for the future, this story reminds me of how precious life is and how one little four year old child, who touched our lives so briefly, but has stayed in our hearts to this day.

Josephine Patricia Mary Mullen – Joene
Born 19 March 1965
Died 31 December 1969

Uncle Jim Mullen

James Mullen – Born 17 September 1927 – Died 23 December 1971. (Aged 44)

Within families there are always siblings that are just that little bit extra close and in my Mother's family, she was especially close to her brother Jim.

Jim was a very pleasant smiling young fella who loved to dress in style and he had a full head of curly Mullen hair – same as my Mother.
Uncle Jim worked in various jobs – mostly with Department of Agriculture, Drainage Division where he was a foreman. He was devoted to his oldest brother George and became his eyes when George became blind during his early years. Jim was witty and musical – he played in Blackwatertown Pipe Band.

Jim married Bridie McCann, from Bogbawn, Killyman on 26 June 1957 and they set up home in Eagerlougher, Loughgall, in a small farm which Jim had inherited from his Great Aunt, Ellen Higgins.

Bridie was a well-known local Nurse and together they raised a family of three boys, Peter, Brian, Seamus and one girl Aideen. Probably because Mammy and Daddy were around the same age as Bridie and Jim, they became even closer and when we were children we went every Friday night to Eagerlougher and the Mullen's came every Sunday to Mullen's Hill. Life was very simple then and we enjoyed lots of home-made fun and played all the usual children's games and particularly enjoyed a made up game of "Jumps", with both sets of parents and anyone else who happened to be around joining in– which we played in our front garden. It involved using an old rope of my Fathers with two "sensible" people holding each end. Everyone, young and old, then lined up and jumped over the rope. It was raised a little higher each time until you were "Out" by not making the jump. Daddy always caused us to scream with laughter when he would jiggle the rope when Mammy or Auntie Bridie came along so invariably they would fail and be out……. I can still hear my Mammy chiding him "Oh Tom!!!".

We had wonderful happy memories growing up with our Mullen cousins and we remain close to this day.

Sadly Uncle Jim died quite unexpectedly in 1971, from a Brain Haemorrhage, which happened while attending a Gaelic football match in Madden, Co Armagh.

He survived for a few days but he died on 23 December and was buried on Christmas morning. The loss to Auntie Bridie and the children was immense – Aideen was only five and the thought of those four wee ones on Christmas morning stayed with us for many years. We still continued to visit; even more so after Jim's death, but the house was always a sombre one and the joy and fun that Jim had brought to the family home was missing for many years.

Auntie Bridie soldered on and became a District Nurse – she was one of the old hand types of Nurses and was widely respected and is still often talked about. She raised her family in Eagerlougher and lived to see them all grown up and settled.

The Phone Box at Tullyroan

These little "Tales" have mostly centred around my Mother and her life and times growing up on Mullen's Hill, Co Armagh. There has been very little about my lovely Father, Tommy McGahan who, although a native of Drumhorrick, Killyman, lived on Mullen's Hill from he and Mammy got married in October 1959 until we all moved back to Killyman in 1976.

Mammy and Daddy met at a dance in Clonmore Hall in the spring of 1954. Mammy was quite taken with this dark handsome young man, who she said was a great dancer, and had a lovely smile, but she was quite surprised when she didn't see him again for several months. Unbeknown to her, Daddy's younger brother Joey McGahan had died during that time, he had Leukaemia and was just 15 years old. This was a terrible blow to Daddy's family as Joey was a beautiful fit young boy. He died in hospital in Magherafelt and Daddy's parents, Frank and Cissie (Sarah) were of course bereft. Daddy always said that they couldn't bear to hear his name mentioned after he died, as they found it too upsetting. Daddy never forgot Joey and spoke about him to us often and he would have liked to have named my brother after him but knew it would be too much of a reminder to his parents and so he was given Joseph as a second name.

Daddy and Mammy married in October 1959 and set up home on the crest of Mullen's Hill in a small house that had belonged to Mammy's uncle Barney. Daddy used to make us laugh by telling us about sitting at the fire one evening and looking up and seeing the stars out through the holes in the roof of the house!!. There was no bathroom or kitchen, just a living room, bedroom and scullery. But it was our first home and he and Mammy made it as cheerful and welcoming as they could. They grew vegetables in the front garden and over the years, Daddy, using all his skills as a bricklayer, renovated the house into a lovely comfortable home – it is still standing and still lived in today.

Among the wonderful neighbours on Mullen's Hill were the McNeice family and my Mother in particular formed a lifelong friendship with Mrs McNeice, Maureen, or as she was always known in our family Mrs Mac. She was the epitome of a good neighbour – friendly, helpful and always there when needed… and Mammy was forever thankful for her.

Mammy had two difficult pregnancies which resulted in miscarriage and stillbirth and fell pregnant again in March 1961. She had to remain in bed for nearly all of the pregnancy and Mrs Mac made sure that both she and Daddy were fed and looked after… she even did the washing for them too.

In December 1961, after a long and difficult pregnancy my mother was brought by ambulance to hospital in Dungannon. In those days the husbands daren't go with their wives and so were left in limbo as to the outcome of the previous nine months! Sometime late on Christmas Eve, which was a Sunday that year, Daddy and Mrs Mac made their way to the public phone box at Tullyroan and there contacted the hospital in Dungannon to enquire tentatively if there was "any news". Mrs Mac often recalls how delighted the look on Daddy's face was to hear that he had a baby daughter and that "Mother and Baby were well". She remembers them both being squeezed into the phone box and her hugging him… I can only imagine the joy and relief.

In a lovely tribute to Mrs Mac, Mammy and Daddy chose her to be my God Mother along with Daddy's youngest brother Dermot as God Father.

While having a birthday on Christmas Eve is not ideal, Mrs Mac never forgot and always on a Christmas Eve afternoon, in the midst of Mammy stuffing the turkey and doing a hundred and one other things, Mrs Mac would arrive with a lovely little birthday present for me… it was the only one that I would receive for many years, as anyone with a Christmas birthday will know.

I was very close to both my parents, and the loss of my father 31 years ago, when he was only 57, was a sore blow. Now that Mammy has gone to be with him I love to think of the two of them, dancing the night away with Mammy looking fine in a summer dress and Daddy looking dapper in a suit and tie, both youthful and full of life and expectations.

Daddy always said that his life changed, for the better, that night … all those years ago…in the phone box in Tullyroan.

Lost on Mullen's Hill

Many years ago, when I was just a little bit of a thing!!! My lovely parents decided that, as I was their first born and ever so precious!! they had better make secure our home and garden - so that I could play outside in relative safety. My father, Tommy, went to great expense in buying and installing strong black iron gates at the front and back of the house…..and they were pronounced a great job indeed and would keep a nation safe. Little did they know that my powers of escapology were much greater than any of them could imagine. For the very next day after they were installed - I went missing!!

Now it being Derrymagone in the early 1960's, there were limited places that I could or would have gone. But a neighbourhood search was mounted for me, with friends and family from Mullen's Hill, Canary and The Ruddery Hill joining in. A great fear at that time was that I would have gone "to the river" which was the River Blackwater that flowed through the meadow fields about a half a mile away. Why they thought I would have gone there - I don't know - but it became a concern and a group of men went off to check out the river banks for a little three year old. My poor mother must have been distraught as I was missing for several hours at this point. It was decided that there was nothing else for it but to call the Police. Talk of kidnapping and abduction were mentioned and local deep wells were also on the list of dreadful mishaps which could have befallen me. My Aunt Nan - ever the practical one - was charged with going to the nearest telephone - probably in McBennett's shop to make the call to summon the Police. She went back to her home - my Mother's home house further down Mullen's Hill, to get her trusty scooter out for the journey and to her delight found a very tired three year old sitting happily on the doorstep cuddled up with Pip, who was Uncle George's very friendly Corgi dog.

I was none the worse for my "ordeal"; however I can't say the same for my poor parents, who spent a further considerable sum putting wire around the sturdy gates so that little monkeys could not climb out through them again! I have no recollection of this incident – but Mammy often remembered it and we laughed about it – but I could still see the fear in her eyes - even after all these years.

The McGahan children remained safe – the gates stayed in place for many years and I can still hear the clang of them opening and closing and I loved Pip all my life - he was the first of many doggy friends.

The Moss's come to Mullen's Hill

Every summer, when we were children, our days were brightened each year by the arrival of the Moss children. These were the grandchildren of our Mullen's Hill neighbours Arthur and Nan Molloy and they came every summer to stay with their grandparents. They lived in Portsmouth, England, which to us seemed to be a wonderful far away, exotic place, where the children all spoke with very posh accents and were a lovely golden brown colour.

The arrival of the Moss children was the highlight of our summer. We never knew exactly when they were arriving and we waited daily, listening for the purr of their Volkswagen Beetle chuffing up Mullen's Hill and then the squeals of delight and the clanging of our gates as the three of them descended on our house and fun and chaos reigned for the next few weeks. I clearly remember their mother, Mary, shouting after them as they sprinted for our house - "You must come in and see your Grandma first ... before going to the McGahan's!!!" But not one of them was listening... I think they enjoyed those summer days as much as we did.

The arrival of Patricia, Bernard and Peter Moss meant that for us - summer time had begun. Days were spent playing ...mostly skipping - yes the boys too, and other games that we made up. We made dens in the garden with old ladders and pieces of wood and Mammy's old eiderdowns and we threatened to sleep all night in them - but we always chickened out when it started to get dark. We loved going for adventures in The Argory. Many boxes of treasure were ceremoniously buried among the trees along the lanes in The Argory. If anyone comes upon an old Rover biscuit tin with our names and the date and other dubious trinkets - please do let me know... there were many of them!!

Mr McGeough Bond, the owner of the estate, would sometimes come upon us when he was out for his afternoon walk... we were a little afraid of him, as we really shouldn't have been there because the estate was private property at that time.... but he was always charming and even gave us sweets once or twice.

My Mother let us bake biscuits and make a terrible mess in her kitchen- but we ate up all our produce with relish. We dressed up as princesses and pirates and acted out plays and scenes on our front street.

The days were long and sunny. We were out from first light until it got dark.

We were never hungry, but always fed, never dirty but always nearly clean, absolutely never bored... there wasn't enough hours in the day for us to accomplish all that we had planned. It wasn't unknown for us to be woken by the clanging of our gates opening around 7.00am - as the Moss children arrived for the day..... Oh ...and the TV was never switched on....!!

We helped the O'Brien's and Uncle George with the bailing of hay - and loved to hitch a ride down to the meadows clinging precariously onto the back of the hay trailer to collect hay bales. On the way back we sat on top of the bales, which were only very dubiously tied and it was great craic altogether if you slipped down between the bales of hay, or even better.....slipped off the trailer onto the lane...... Health & Safety... Never heard of it!!

Those glorious summers lasted well into our teens - they came to an end when Arthur and Nan passed away and the holidays to Mullen's Hill became less frequent. Our friendship has continued over the years. Patricia and I have always kept in touch and we keep each other up to date with the news of the boys. We met up again in person two years ago when she was back on Mullen's Hill for a visit and we were able to slot back into that familiar friendship that only children who grew up together can have.

When we meet it is like we have gone back to those days on Mullen's Hill - we are on the same wave length and we can laugh and remember the things we did and the fun we had. It is like an invisible thread from our childhood which weaves through us all.

We were lucky to have had such an idyllic time and blessed with such friends to light up our lives when we were growing up on Mullen's Hill.

And finally……….thank you to everyone who took the time to buy this book - I hope you enjoyed reading it. It has been my pleasure to put these short stories together and I will forever be indebted to my late mother Brigid, not only for her clear and wonderful recollection of growing up on Mullen's Hill but also the very fond memories of the many lovely times we spent together remembering and recalling these little "Tales".